BASEBALL

A Book of Quips and Quotes

BASEBALL

A Book of Quips and Quotes

Ariel Books

Andrews and McMeel
Kansas City

ISBN:0-8362-3112-0

Library of Congress Catalog Card Number: 94-74182

CONTENTS

Rough Special

INTRODUCTION

Why do more words of wit and wisdom come from baseball than from any other sport (or perhaps any other field) in the United States? First, the leisurely pace of baseball allows players, managers, fans, and writers more time for reflection. Granted, football also has a lot of time between plays, but most football players use that time to regain consciousness and to try to remember who and where they are.

Second, the nature of the game lends itself to philosophizing. Baseball thrusts upon its players, managers, and fans the great questions regarding the meaning of life and the definition of success. For it is the only sport that encourages acceptance of failure as an integral part of success. No baseball manager would ever echo the words of football coach Vince Lombardi, who said, "Winning isn't everything; it's the only thing." Baseball players and coaches know better. After all, the best teams and pitchers lose at least one out of three games, while the best hitters only *succeed* one out of three times.

Finally, the game builds character. Even baseball's superstars spent several years in the minor leagues. And a person would either have to be plain crazy or crazy for baseball to travel dusty roads in overcrowded buses for virtually no pay day after day simply to get to the next ball game. Those who actually make it to the major leagues become symbols of the American dream: they're the best in their field, they're making money, and they're doing what they love to do.

THE PLAYERS SPEAK

Baseball can build you up to the sky one day and the next day you have to climb a stepladder to look up to a snake.

—*Johnny Pesky*

Trying to sneak a pitch past Hank Aaron is like trying to sneak the sunrise past a rooster.

—*Joe Adcock*

Nothing makes a pitcher feel more secure
than the sight of his teammates
circling the bases
during a ball game.

—*Jim Brosnan*

You know, I saw it all happen, from beginning to end. But sometimes I still can't believe what I saw: this nineteen-year-old kid, crude, poorly educated, only lightly brushed by the social veneer we call civilization, gradually transformed into the idol of American youth and the symbol of baseball the world over—a man loved by more people and with an intensity of feeling that perhaps has never been equaled before or since.

—*Harry Hooper* (on Babe Ruth)

Once he threw me a spitter at first base to pick off a runner. The ball sank a foot and I dropped it. When I threw it back to him it was still wet and sank again. The runners advanced a base and I got an error!

—*Orlando Cepeda* (on Gaylord Perry)

When you're 21, you're a prospect. When you're 30, you're a suspect.

—*Jim McGlothin*

Winning makes you happy all day.

—*Jimmy Wynn*

You're only as smart as your ERA.

—*Jim Bouton*

All you have to do is pick up a baseball. It begs to you: throw me. If you took a year to design an object to hurl, you'd end up with that little spheroid: small enough to nestle in your fingers but big enough to have some heft, lighter than a rock but heavier than a hunk of wood. Its even, neat stitching, laced into the leather's slippery white surface, gives your fingers a purchase. A baseball was made to throw. It's almost irresistible.

—*Dave Dravecky*

Natural grass is a wonderful thing for little bugs and sinkerball pitchers.

—*Dan Quisenberry*

I just pick it up and throw it. He hit it. They scored. We didn't. That's it. It's over. It's history. OK?

—*Vida Blue*

Whitey and I figured out once that each year I hit about fifteen long outs at Yankee Stadium that would have been home runs at Ebbets Field. In my eighteen years I would have gotten 270 additional home runs if I'd been a Dodger.

—*Mickey Mantle*

On artificial turf, the ball says, "Catch me." On grass, it says, "Look out, sucker."

—*Greg Pryor*

I was standing in right field. At first I thought it was another of my migraines, but it was just an earthquake.

> —*José Canseco* (on the 1989 World Series earthquake)

I'm not going to ask for more money, I'll just wait and let them come and insist I take a raise.

> —*Bo Belinsky*

We know we're better than this, but we can't prove it.

—*Tony Gwynn* (on a Padres losing streak)

To the fierce, ardent leather-lunged professional fan, baseball is life itself, a motive for breathing, the yeast that helps his spirit, as well as his gorge, rise.

—*Jim Bouton*

I figured baseball would be just as good as the overalls factory. I knew I would go as far as my arm would take me. Nobody would help me. I knew that if you want a helping hand in this world look at the end of your arm.

—*Bo Belinsky*

Blind people come to the park just to listen to him pitch.

—*Reggie Jackson* (on Tom Seaver)

I became a good pitcher when I stopped trying to make them miss the ball and started trying to make them hit it.

—*Sandy Koufax*

The best thing about baseball is that you can do something about yesterday tomorrow.

—*Manny Trillo*

They throw the ball, I hit it; they hit the ball, I catch it.

—*Willie Mays*

Was it difficult leaving the *Titanic?*

—*Sal Bando* (on being asked how he felt about leaving the Oakland A's)

I'd like to thank the good Lord for making me a Yankee.

—*Joe DiMaggio*

Bob Gibson is the luckiest pitcher I ever saw. He always pitches when the other team doesn't score any runs.

—*Tim McCarver*

Candlestick Park is the gross error in the history of major league baseball. Designed, at a corner table in Lefty O'Doul's, a Frisco saloon, by two politicians and an itinerant ditchdigger, the ballpark slants toward the bay—in fact, it *slides* toward the bay and before long will be under water, which is the best place for it.

—*Jim Brosnan*

Baseball is like a poker game. Nobody wants to quit when he's losing; nobody wants you to quit when you're ahead.

—*Jackie Robinson*

Jimmy Connors plays two tennis matches and winds up with $850,000, and Muhammad Ali fights one bout and winds up with five million bucks. Me, I play 190 games—if you count exhibitions—and *I'm* overpaid!

—*Johnny Bench*

Experience is a hard teacher because she gives the test first, the lesson afterward.

—*Vernon Law*

Baseball, to me, is still the national pastime because it is a summer game. I feel that almost all Americans are summer people, that summer is what they think of when they think of their childhood. I think it stirs up an incredible emotion within people.

—*Steve Busby*

Gee, it's lonesome in the outfield. It's hard to keep awake with nothing to do.

—*Babe Ruth*

Pitching is . . . the art of instilling fear.

—*Sandy Koufax*

Don't forget to swing hard in case you hit the ball.

—*Woodie Held*

Spread out, guys, so they can't get all of us with one shot.

—*Frank Sullivan* (on seeing a crowd during a losing streak)

Baseball is the only field of endeavor in which a man can succeed three times out of ten and be considered a good performer.

—*Ted Williams*

I didn't come to New York to be a star. I brought my star with me.

—*Reggie Jackson*

I know, but I had a better year than Hoover.

—*Babe Ruth* (responding to a reporter who pointed out that his 1930 salary of $80,000 was higher than the president's $75,000)

The way to catch a knuckleball is to wait until it stops rolling and then to pick it up.

—*Bob Uecker*

Why pitch nine innings when you can get just as famous pitching two?

—*Sparky Lyle*

Don't look back. Something may be gaining on you.

—*Satchel Paige*

It's tomorrow that counts. So you worry all the time. It never ends. Lord, baseball is a worrying thing.

—*Stan Coveleski*

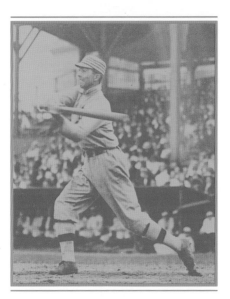

It starts out like a baseball and when it gets to the plate it looks like a marble.

—*Hack Wilson* (on Satchel Paige's fastball)

Never at a loss for words, Paige had this response: "You must be talking about my slow ball. My fastball looks like a fish egg."

The two most important things in life are good friends and a strong bullpen.

—*Bob Lemon*

I found a delivery in my flaw.

—*Dan Quisenberry*

Don't quit until every base is uphill.

—*Babe Ruth*

This winter I'm working out every day, throwing at a wall. I'm 11-0 against the wall.

—*Jim Bouton* (remarking on his comeback attempt)

Do they leave it there during games?

—*Bill "Spaceman" Lee* (upon first seeing the Green Monster, Fenway's 37-foot-high left-field wall)

I've heard of guys going 0 for 15, or 0 for 25, but I was 0 for July.

—*Bob Aspromonte*

This team, it all flows from me. I've got to keep it going. I'm the straw that stirs the drink.

—*Reggie Jackson*

I never seemed to feel as hostile toward the knuckleball when I listened to the French-speaking broadcasters in Montreal, who call it *le papillon,* the butterfly. You can't feel as bad about a passed ball knowing it was caused by *le papillon.* Striking out because you didn't hit *le papillon* makes you feel like you should get an award from some environmental group.

—*Joe Garagiola*

YOGI

A nickel ain't worth a dime anymore.

Baseball is 90 percent mental. The other half is physical.

He can run anytime he wants. I'm giving him the red light.

I got a touch of pantomine poisoning.

I wish I had an answer to that question because I'm getting tired of answering that question.

It gets late early out here.

It's so crowded nobody goes there anymore.

—(on Toots Shor's restaurant)

We made too many wrong mistakes.

You can observe a lot by watching.

Our similarities are different.

—*Dale Berra* (on comparisons to his father, Yogi)

OUT OF THE MOUTHS OF MANAGERS (& UMPS)

The secret of managing is to keep the guys who hate you away from the guys who are undecided.

—*Casey Stengel*

A full mind is an empty bat.

—*Branch Rickey*

A lot of the calls (by an umpire) are guesses. They have to be. How can you really tell, for example, when a ball is trapped rather than caught by an outfielder? The gloves today are so big they can cover the side of a building. So you make the call and hope they don't show you up on the instant replay. With balls and strikes, it's impossible to get them right all the time. I mean, every major-league pitch moves some way or other. None go straight, not even the fastballs. And the batters often can't do any better than the umpires.

—*Ron Luciano,* umpire

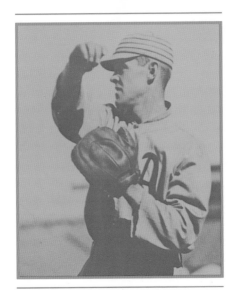

That's for birds to eat. I'm afraid my players might start molting or going to the bathroom on newspapers.

—*Rocky Bridges* (when asked about players eating sunflower seeds)

Don't cut my throat, I may want to do that later myself.

—*Casey Stengel* (to a barber, allegedly)

At the end of this season, they're gonna tear this place down. The way you're pitchin', that right-field section will be gone already.

—*Casey Stengel* (to pitcher Tracy Stallard)

The pay is good, it keeps you out in the fresh air and sunshine, and you can't beat the hours.

—*Tim Hurst,* umpire

Baseball is almost the only orderly thing in a very unorderly world. If you get three strikes, even the best lawyer in the world can't get you off.

—*Bill Veeck*

You're expected to be perfect the day you start, and then improve.

—*Ed Vargo,* supervisor of umpires

It is a game to be savored rather than taken in gulps.

—*Bill Veeck*

Any umpire who claims he has never missed a play is . . . well, an umpire.

—*Ron Luciano,* umpire

Not really. They lean towards cash.

—*Bill Veeck* (when asked if free agents lean toward big cities)

Man may penetrate the outer reaches of the universe, he may solve the very secret of eternity itself, but for me, the ultimate human experience is to witness the flawless execution of a hit-and-run.

—*Branch Rickey*

Managing a ball club is the most vulnerable job in the world. . . . If you don't win, you're going to be fired. If you do win, you've only put off the day you're going to be fired. And no matter what you do, you're going to be second-guessed. The manager is the only person in the ballpark who has to call it right now. Everybody else can call it after it's over.

—*Leo Durocher*

When I played, you came to spring training with a ten-pound winter beer belly on, and you ran about thirty wind sprints and you sweated with a sweat jacket and you got yourself in condition. Now the players do Nautilus all winter, they play racquetball, they swim, they exercise, and they come to spring training looking like Tarzan.

—*Jim Leyland*

Ballplayers are a superstitious breed, nobody more than I, and while you are winning you'd murder anybody who tried to change your sweat-shirt, let alone your uniform.

—*Leo Durocher*

Umpire's heaven is a place where he works third base every game. Home is where the heartache is.

—*Ron Luciano*, umpire

I occasionally get birthday cards from fans. But it's often the same message: they hope it's my last.

—*Al Forman*, National League umpire

OTHERS HAVE THEIR SAY

When I was a small boy in Kansas, a friend of mine and I went fishing and as we sat there in the warmth of the summer afternoon on a river bank, we talked about what we wanted to do when we grew up. I told him that I wanted to be a real major league baseball player, a genuine professional like Honus Wagner. My friend said that he'd like to be president of the United States. Neither of us got our wish.

—*Dwight D. Eisenhower*

It breaks your heart. It is designed to break your heart. The game begins in the spring, when everything else begins again, and it blossoms in the summer, filling the afternoons and evenings, and then as soon as the chill rains come, it stops and leaves you to face the fall alone.

—*Bart Giamatti*

How 'bout that, sports fans?
—*Mel Allen,* signature line

World Series week indicates that baseball is one of America's major disturbances.

—*Bugs Baer*

Every day in every way, baseball gets fancier. A few more years and they'll be playing on oriental rugs.

—*Russell Baker*

Beatles, shmeetles, we have the Mets.

—*Shea Stadium banner*

To err is human, to forgive is a Mets fan.

—*Polo Grounds banner,* 1962

Fanaticism? No. Writing is exciting and baseball is like writing.

—*Marianne Moore*

One of the chief duties of the fan is to engage in arguments with the man behind him. This department has been allowed to run down fearfully.

—*Robert Benchley*

A hot dog at the ballpark is better than steak at the Ritz.

—*Humphrey Bogart*

Whoever dreamed that Pete Rose, who's given us such childish pleasure, would now give us such deeply adult pain?

—*Thomas Boswell*

Every member of our baseball team at West Point became a general: this proves the value of team sports for the military.

—*Omar Bradley*

Ideally, the umpire should combine the integrity of a Supreme Court Justice, the physical agility of an acrobat, the endurance of Job, and the imperturbability of Buddha.

—*Time Magazine*

Baseball isn't statistics, it's Joe DiMaggio rounding second base.

—*Jimmy Breslin*

It's the fans that need spring training. You gotta get 'em interested. Wake 'em up. Let 'em know that their season is coming, the good times are gonna roll.

—*Harry Caray*

The poet or storyteller who feels that he is competing with a superb double play in the World Series is a lost man. One would not want as a reader a man who did not appreciate the finesse of a double play.

—*John Cheever*

I find baseball fascinating. It strikes me as a native American ballet—a totally different dance form. Nearly every move in baseball—the windup, the pitch, the motion of the infielders—is different from other games. Next to a triple play, baseball's double play is the most exciting and graceful thing in sports.

—*Alistair Cooke*

Two-thirds of the earth is covered by water, the other one-third is covered by Garry Maddox.

—*Ralph Kiner,* Mets announcer

Baseball players are the weirdest of all. I think it's all that organ music.

—*Peter Gent*

The sneer has gone from Casey's lip, his
    teeth are clenched in hate;
He pounds with cruel violence his bat
    upon the plate.
And now the pitcher holds the ball, and
    now he lets it go,
And now the air is shattered by the force
    of Casey's blow.
Oh! somewhere in this favored land the
    sun is shining bright;
The band is playing somewhere, and
    somewhere hearts are light;
And somewhere men are laughing, and
    somewhere children shout;

ut there is no joy in Mudville—mighty
Casey has struck out.

—*Ernest Lawrence Thayer,*
   Casey at the Bat

TWO DREAM TEAMS

The subject of countless hours of debate: Who were the best ever to play the game? You may disagree, but the twenty players on this list are certainly among the all-time greats.

	NATIONAL LEAGUE	**AMERICAN LEAGUE**
C	Johnny Bench	Yogi Berra
1B	Willie McCovey	Lou Gehrig
2B	Joe Morgan	Eddie Collins
3B	Mike Schmidt	George Brett
SS	Honus Wagner	Luke Appling
OF	Stan Musial	Ted Williams
OF	Willie Mays	Ty Cobb
OF	Hank Aaron	Babe Ruth
RHP	Christy Mathewson	Walter Johnson
LHP	Warren Spahn	Lefty Grove

The text of this book was set in
American Garamond and the Display
was set in Rockwell Bold Condensed by
Snap-Haus Graphics, Dumont, NJ.

Book design by
Diane Stevenson/Snap-Haus Graphics